SEE IN 3D

CREEPY CREATURES

SEYMOUR SIMON

SCHOLASTIC INC.

New York Toronto London Auckland Sydney
Mexico City New Delhi Hong Kong Buenos Aires

To my grandson Joel,
Teenage Years, here they come,
from Grandpa Seymour

ACKNOWLEDGMENTS
Special thanks to Ron Labbe of Studio 3-D for his expertise and 3-D photo conversions. Thanks also to Alison Kolani for her skillful copyediting. The author is grateful to David Reuther and Ellen Friedman for their editorial and design suggestions, as well as their enthusiasm for this project. Also, many thanks to Gina Shaw, Suzanne Nelson, and Carla Siegel at Scholastic Inc., for their generous help and support.

PHOTO CREDITS
Front cover: © Photographer's Choice/Getty Images; title page, pages 3, 5, 6, 13, 14–15, 17, 18, 20, and 24: © Mark Blum; page 4: © David Maitland/Getty Images; page 7: © Altrento Nature/Getty Images; page 8: © Millard H. Sharp/Photo Researchers, Inc.; page 9: © Rod Planck/Photo Researchers, Inc.; pages 10–11: © 3D Vision International; pages 22–23: © Dr. Tony Brain/Photo Researchers, Inc.; back cover: © David Burder/Getty Images

Book design: Ellen Friedman

ISBN 0-439-77703-8

12 11 10 9 8 7 6 5 4 3 2 1   6 7 8 9 10 11/0

Printed in the U.S.A.
First printing, March 2006

The creepy creatures in this book are strange-looking insects, spiders, and other small animals. The number of insects on Earth is enormous, 200 million times greater than the human population. Insects are found in every part of the world, from icy polar regions to the hot sands of tropical deserts. Many of them are so small that we don't even know they are there.

Shield bugs are common in most gardens and country places. The stinkbug is another name for this creepy crawler. It leaves a trail of stinky liquid wherever it goes.

Ants are amazing. An ant worker can carry 20 to 50 times its own weight. If you were strong like an ant, you could pick up a cow and carry it around. Ants run very fast on their six three-jointed legs. If you had legs like an ant, you could run as fast as a racehorse. There are more than 10,000 different kinds of ants known worldwide. In fact, ants outnumber people by more than a million to one.

An ant has large, strong jaws that open and shut sideways like a pair of scissors. Ants don't chew and eat solid food. Instead, they swallow the juices they squeeze from foods and throw away the dry part. An ant has two stomachs, one to feed itself and another one that stores food. The ant later spits up the stored food and shares it with other ants in its nest.

There are more than 350,000 different kinds of beetles that are known and many more kinds that have yet to be discovered. Beetles live all over the world, in places like deserts, mountains, rain forests, and even underwater in streams and ponds. A beetle hatches from an egg and becomes a larva, also called a grub. Beetle larvae usually look like worms or sometimes tiny lizards. After a beetle molts many times, or sheds its skin, its final layer of outer skin hardens. Then the beetle turns into a pupa that grows into an adult, like the Rhinoceros beetle shown below.

Weevils are common kinds of beetles with long snouts or beaks that they use to bore into plants. Their jaws are at the end of their snouts. The giant weevil shown on the left is about three inches long and feeds on plants and crops. The most serious insect threat to crops in the United States is the boll weevil, which feeds on cotton plants.

Caterpillars look completely different from butterflies or moths, but they are really the same insect. Caterpillars hatch from tiny eggs the size of a speck of dust that were laid by butterflies and moths. Then they grow to more than 27,000 times their original size. If you weighed 7 pounds at birth and grew at the same rate as a caterpillar, you would weigh close to 200,000 pounds, about as much as 20 big elephants.

Most caterpillars shed their skins five times as they grow. When caterpillars shed their final skins, they become pupae. The outer skin of the butterfly pupa hardens to form a chrysalis. The moth caterpillar spins a silken cocoon and becomes a pupa inside the cocoon. Within a chrysalis or a cocoon, the pupa is undergoing an amazing change. It is becoming a butterfly or a moth. When the adult emerges, like the fully grown moth below, it will lay eggs, and the life cycle will begin once again.

Damselflies and dragonflies are closely related insects. Dragonflies are usually bigger and heavier than damselflies. Also, a dragonfly's hind wings are bigger than its forewings. Damselflies, like the one on the right, have two sets of wings that are the same size. Both insects begin life underwater, hatching from eggs. The larvae, or nymphs, are deadly hunters, feeding on tadpoles and small fish. Some kinds live underwater for a few months, while others take years to become adults. At last, they crawl up a plant stem or onto a rock and begin to change. The outer skin of the nymph cracks and splits open, and an adult dragonfly or damselfly comes out.

As soon as their wings dry and their bodies harden, the adults take to the air and begin hunting for flying insects. They can easily fly straight up or down, hover in midair, dart sideways, and change directions suddenly at speeds up to 30 miles per hour. They have excellent eyesight and can spot prey, such as a mosquito, from 100 feet away.

Most insects have four wings, but flies have only two. In place of a second pair of wings, flies have halteres, small knoblike structures used for balancing. A fly beats its wings 200 times a second—three times faster than a hummingbird.

There are 120,000 different kinds of flies, ranging in size from tiny ones about the size of a pinhead to large flies three inches long. This green bottle fly is medium-sized, about a half inch long. Bottle flies, houseflies, and many other flies can carry disease germs. A single fly can carry up to 2,000,000 germs on its body.

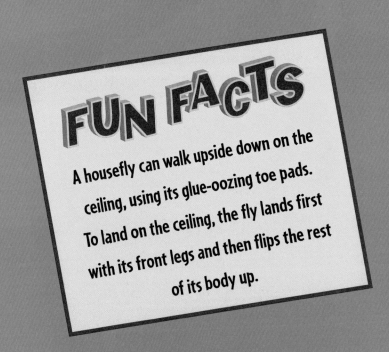

FUN FACTS

A housefly can walk upside down on the ceiling, using its glue-oozing toe pads. To land on the ceiling, the fly lands first with its front legs and then flips the rest of its body up.

Leaf insects are the same shape and color as the leaves of the plants they live on. As they move, leaf insects can even change color to match their new surroundings. If you disturb them, they sway gently like a leaf caught in a breeze. Or they may drop to the ground, pull their legs into their body, and remain very still and hard to spot. If a bird grabs them, they can lose a leg and later grow a replacement.

Leaf insects are large, four or more inches long. They are most common in rain forests in Southeast Asia. Some leaf insects are kept as pets. Walking sticks, which look like twigs, belong to this same group of insects. Some walking sticks are over one foot in length, making them the longest insects in the world.

Millipedes are long, wormlike animals with many body segments. Each body segment has two pairs of legs attached to it. Millipedes, like the one shown on the right, are sometimes called thousand-leggers, but the actual number of their legs is much less than that. They vary in length from less than 1 inch to more than 2 inches. Centipedes are similar to millipedes, but they have one pair of legs attached to each body segment instead of two pairs.

Millipedes usually live outdoors under moist, decaying leaves or dead trees. They feed on dead plant material. Sometimes they can be found together in large numbers, especially after heavy rains or as the weather gets cooler in the autumn. Millipedes climb walls easily and can enter a house through any small opening.

FUN FACTS

The most legs found on a single millipede is about 750.

Mosquitoes are insects that bite and draw blood from warm-blooded animals and people. Only female mosquitoes bite. Mosquitoes also inject their saliva into the victim. In that way, they transmit certain diseases such as malaria, yellow fever, or the West Nile virus. The mosquito is responsible for more deaths worldwide than any other insect.

Mosquitoes zoom in on animals like heat-seeking missiles. They can smell their prey from more than 30 feet away. When they get closer, they can spot a moving target from 18 feet. When they are 10 feet away, mosquitoes use very sensitive heat detectors located on their antennas to find warm blood near the surface of their prey's skin.

You are more likely to be a target for mosquitoes if you eat certain kinds of sweet fruits, or if you use perfume, scented soaps, or body lotion. If you are bitten, try not to scratch a mosquito bite—it only makes the itching worse.

FUN FACTS

The buzz a mosquito makes is caused by its wings beating 500 times a second.

Scorpions are poisonous animals—they have long bodies tipped with a venomous stinger. Scorpions live around the world in deserts, forests, grasslands, and caves. They have even been found under snow-covered rocks high in mountains. About 90 different kinds of scorpions live in the United States, mostly west of the Mississippi River. Despite their scary reputation, only one kind of scorpion in the United States has poison powerful enough to kill a human being. It lives in the deserts of the Southwest.

Scorpions range in size from 3 or 4 inches to more than 8 inches long. Scorpions are active at night, feeding on insects, spiders, and even smaller lizards, snakes, and mice. They have a pair of pincers and four pairs of legs. The pincers are covered by fine hairs that sense vibrations in the air around nearby prey. The tips of a scorpion's legs can also detect vibrations in the ground.

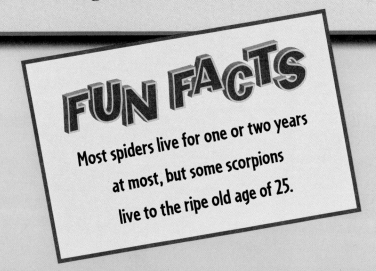

FUN FACTS

Most spiders live for one or two years at most, but some scorpions live to the ripe old age of 25.

Spiders have two body parts, the head and the abdomen, with eight legs attached to the abdomen. They have two large jaws, and most have eight eyes. Even though they have a lot of eyes, spiders have poor eyesight and can see clearly only from a few inches away.

All spiders make silk, but not all spiders make webs. Spiders use their silk to wrap prey and keep it from escaping. A spider doesn't chew its food. It bites its prey and injects venom that turns the tissue of the prey into a liquid. You might say that spiders eat insect soup.

Robber flies are hunters. They have powerful wings and strong legs that can catch insects in flight. Its large compound eyes and the dense bristles on its head make the robber fly look like a mini-monster!

People could not survive without insects. We would not have fruits, vegetables, and plants that depend on insect pollination. There would be no honey, silk, or other insect products. Dead trees and animals would cover the ground without insects to hurry their decay. Birds and other animals that depend on insects for food would perish. Insects are an important part of the web of life.